# Don't Die Broke

## Easy Steps on How to Save, Invest, and Build Your Wealth

by R. L. Borom in collaboration with R. T. Borom

# Table Of Contents

"A journey of a thousand miles begins with a single step."

*LAO-TZU, Chinese philosopher*

# PREFACE

Take a moment to digest the following statistics:

- **20% of American wealth is controlled by 0.1 percent of our population.**[1] That's right. About 170,000 families in a country of roughly 330 million people control that much of our total wealth. **Think! That's one-tenth of one percent!**

- **The top 1% of our population controls 39% of American wealth.**[1] That leaves only 61% to be divided among the remaining 99% of our population.

- **The top 10% of our population controls 74% of American wealth.**[2] In other words, the bottom 90% of Americans combined only control 26% of the total wealth.

- Barely one third ($1/3$) of American families in the bottom 50% of earners own stocks, according to the Federal Reserve. On the other hand, nearly 94% of the top income group owned stocks in 2016.

- **Less than one third ($1/3$) of Americans, ages 18 to 29, owned stocks** on average between 2009 and 2017, according to a Gallup survey released during April 2019. Nearly **two-thirds ($2/3$) of Americans between 30 and 64 own stocks.**[2]

If you combined all of the bottom half of the population (50%), they have a negative net worth. This means, to put it bluntly, they are FLAT BROKE!

*Which one of these groups do you belong to?*

- Do you notice an investment trend that is contributing to the worsening inequality in America? Which investment vehicle do the majority of the wealthy own to grow their money? Hint - STOCKS!!

Let me show you how you can save, invest and build wealth in the stock market - even if you have little money or no investing experience.

# INTRODUCTION
## The Journey of Hard Knocks!

**L**ike the majority of us, I have struggled with discovering methods to save and invest money to help me to enjoy a brighter future. I vividly recall the many years spent toiling away, trying lots of different methods to build a better future for my family.

Even though I seemed to possess an inborn sense of saving for the future, I lacked true direction. I lacked even basic knowledge about investing money.

For example, my wife and I decided to invest $30 per month in a mutual fund and this was shortly after the birth of our third child. We were struggling financially but, even so, we agreed that we needed to sacrifice even more to be better prepared for the family's future.

What did we do? We invested the $30 in a mutual fund on which, unknowingly, we did no research other than it appeared to be sponsored by a reputable insurance company. Big mistake! During our six-year investment period, we made zero dollars ("0") in profit.

Given our ignorance, we were fortunate to have done that well. By the way, being ignorant does not mean that you are dumb or stupid, it simply means that you don't know or that you are lacking in knowledge.

After dabbling about for several more years, buying mixtures of Certificates of Deposit (CDs), U.S. savings bonds, advertised best paying bank savings accounts, and miscellaneous mutual funds and stocks, we determined that our saving and investment efforts were doing poorly.

# Why Pay to Bankroll Someone Else's Greed?

Our next step involved acquiring a financial advisor. Initially, matters appeared to be going well. His early efforts seemed to be directed toward improving our investment portfolio. However, after a few years, I began to take more of an in-depth look at the investments in which he was placing us.

For the sake of brevity, I'll list a few of the negative ones, many of which involved large commissions (generally about 8%) for the advisor. How about annuities, whole life insurance policies, questionable specialty companies (the leasing of airplane engines, real estate investments, etc.)? There were just a few

solid mutual funds from a major mutual fund company (Fidelity). Obviously, we didn't feel very secure.

As I continued to read the reports issued for the
various investments, I became more and more aware
of the lack of growth in many of our accounts.

In a few cases, some of the accounts had been
manipulated for the advisor to drain a small percent-
age more of profit. Are you surprised to discover that
we stopped all contact with the advisor?

You may have guessed my next move. After
mentally kicking myself for having been so trusting
and reliant on others to invest for me, I decided to
begin learning how to self-manage our investment
portfolio.

# How "Don't Die Broke" Can Help You Build Wealth

There was always the basic question of: How could I adopt a reasonably quick, fairly painless and accurate method to save and invest?

**Don't Die Broke** is designed to help you develop an efficient savings and investment system. This system will remove a great deal of the mental struggle, which far too often accompanies attempts to save and invest. It really doesn't have to be that way.

Any concepts presented are based on your ability to gradually improve your saving and investment skills, as you experience the growth of your portfolio. Your results will be natural outcomes of your efforts and based on my experiences, are far LESS difficult to achieve than you might imagine.

Investing is not an impossible challenge or a huge mystery. Increased learning simply comes with the study and practice of investing your money.

# About the Author

I have many life experiences that led me to write "Don't Die Broke" in collaboration with my son, R. T. Borom. After serving in the U.S. Air Force, I raised three children with my wife of 50 years while working my way through college as a school janitor. Earning my bachelor's and master's degrees, my professional career spanned positions in higher education, corporate America and real estate investing.

While in corporate America, I studied the use of behavior modification to change behavior positively. Of course, changing your ECONOMIC BEHAVIOR is of critical importance in developing a successful savings and investment plan.

Despite numerous setbacks and the hard-earned lessons and disillusionments that came from the many attempts to succeed in investing and growing my hard-earned money, I PERSEVERED. Giving up simply wasn't in my DNA.

With this in mind, the information contained in this book represents some of the best lessons learned from my life experiences to ease your path in building wealth.

# My Purpose

I am hopeful that the information included in this book will be of great help to you in developing your savings and investment plan. I also sincerely hope that it will assist you in avoiding much of the pain and monetary loss that I encountered from my earlier learning experiences.

**My purpose is to give you, the reader, simple and short methods for saving and investing your hard-earned money.** Hopefully, I have listed these methods in a manner that will be readable, easy to use and most of all, helpful in changing your savings and investment experience.

# Summary

No matter the amount of money you have, it's time to get started saving and investing. Changing and controlling your ECONOMIC BEHAVIOR is a crucial part of your success. Once you get started, staying with your plan is essential; **DISCIPLINE** is the key.

Greater knowledge of investment skills will come with experience and practice.

Watching your plan succeed will encourage you to continue. ***Following these simple steps will help make you a winner!*** LET'S GET STARTED!

# 1

# WHAT DOES IT TAKE FOR YOU TO BECOME A SAVVY INVESTOR?

Changing your economic behavior is not as difficult as you think. When we speak of building your savings and investments, forget your past images of needing thousands of dollars to begin to do so. **Think instead of building one small step at a time.**

Thinking in terms of amassing a large amount of money to start building wealth, will only lead to frustration on your part.

**DID YOU KNOW:** For many people in the bottom 50% of income earners, a $400 emergency could possibly create a serious problem for them.

# Changing Behavior (Habits)

Don't believe that one of the most difficult habits to change is "not saving." Some of the examples that I will give you later will clearly demonstrate that saving is much like breathing air in and out. Once you set up the methods to start saving and investing, it becomes as automatic as breathing. You become accustomed to a pattern that repeats itself over and over. Remember, it's the repetition that's going to grow your wealth (money).

**Most of us are comfortable with our old habits or patterns of behavior. But remember the old saying: "If you always do what you always did, you will always get what you always got."** In other words, if you currently feel that you need to change your savings habits (behavior), you must change your thinking and saving strategy right away.

**EXAMPLE:** After examining my past behavior, I realized that I had fallen into the mental trap of thinking that someone or something out there (a bank, government bonds, an investment or insurance company, a financial advisor, etc.) would automatically spare me from having to make my own decisions about saving and investing my money.

Even though all of these investment possibilities may have a place in your portfolio, only you can determine your starting point.

Establishing your starting point gets you involved early in the development of your savings and investment plan. Most importantly, it gives you a feeling of control and makes it much easier for you to add further knowledge about investing in your plan as it is acquired.

**Changing your behavior (old habits) <u>does</u> <u>not</u> require that you become unbelievably strong. It only requires that you undertake an immediate assessment or review of your current financial state - and take action!**

You will be surprised at how little time such an effort takes. You don't have to do this assessment all at once but can do it over a short time or as thoughts about your various spending habits occur to you. This is critical to your success. This is your starting point!

In the following chapters, I will provide a spreadsheet for you to enter your income and expenses for your budget.

# Summary

**Throw out your old feelings that building wealth can only happen by having huge amounts of money to invest.** This only leads to frustration and makes you unable to act.

Instead, get ready to:

- **Make saving and investing as easy as breathing!**
- Begin an immediate review of your income and expenses.
- Review your income, determine how and where you are spending your money, and establish a budget.
- Establish your starting point.
- Make and keep a written or digital record of your expenses and projected savings.

## 2

# SHOULD YOU SET UP AND FOLLOW A SAVINGS & INVESTMENT SCHEDULE?

**A**bsolutely! Consider your present circumstances. How much are you earning a day, week or month? **Start small. Could you reasonably save five dollars a week, ten dollars a week, twenty dollars a week, or more?** Regardless of the amount selected, you are on your way to establishing a sound savings and investment program. **The key is to stay focused!**

At this point, I would strongly recommend that you NOT attach your debit or credit cards to your savings and investment accounts. Doing so makes it too easy to quickly withdraw your money. This is self-defeating.

Why build your savings and investment accounts if the money can be so easily withdrawn or spent on a whim or in a careless moment of desire? After all, you are building for your future security!

**How can you build a house if you are constantly destroying its foundation?**

If you use a credit card, be certain to avoid unnecessary or needless purchases. It's just too easy to charge purchases on the spur-of the moment. Plus, the interest rates charged on credit card debt will destroy your best attempts to save and you will find yourself caught up in a never-ending cycle of debt.

Please note that you must **review your spending habits** (budget) and weed out as many of the daily, weekly, and monthly (unnecessary) expenses that are forcing you to believe that you cannot establish a solid savings plan. Again, **I suggest that you use a writing pad, computer or phone app to record your findings.**

A critical part of your plan involves establishing a living expense budget. This is a weekly or monthly amount set aside from your paycheck to pay for your actual day-to-day living expenses. Next, you'll have to decide how much you could place in your projected savings fund and investment fund.

The savings fund (to cover present and future emergency living expenses) would be separate from your investment fund, so that you can purchase or invest in index funds (stocks) through mutual fund companies.

These need not be unusually large amounts, as long as you identify specific amounts and maintain a consistent habit of keeping these amounts as separate funds. These separate funds will protect you from having to raid your investment account when unexpected expenses arise.

You should now be in the process of setting up three accounts:

- Your budget for actual LIVING EXPENSES.

- Your savings budget for EMERGENCIES.

- Your INVESTMENT budget to purchase index funds.

**To set up your living expense budget**, consider such things as how many nights you dine out, how many lattes you purchase each week, fast food snacks, excessive streaming of programs or how much is spent on unneeded items (clothing, shoes, entertainment, etc...).

**Taking a home-packed lunch to work is just one of the great ways to start saving.** Cooking more meals at home can easily save $10 to $20, or more per week. Cutting any of these unnecessary expenses is enough to start a solid savings & investment program.

No, I am not suggesting that you deprive yourself of all of life's pleasures. But you should seriously review those expenses that may prevent you from establishing a firmly grounded savings & investment program. When you do so, **you will discover that starting such a program may be easily within your grasp.**

**REMEMBER:** It isn't the size of the amount you start with but the hard, cold fact that you have identified an amount and started. **Just do it!!!**

By determining what your UNNECESSARY EX-PENSES are, you can also determine your NECESSARY EXPENSES.

Necessary expenses are those which you must pay to successfully survive. For instance, rent or mortgage payments, auto payments, smartphones, gasoline, bus or train fare, food, utilities, insurance, medical bills, student loan payments, credit card payments, etc. Such items make up your list of necessary expenses that must be paid consistently.

# Summary (Your Homework!)

1. Establish your BUDGET amount for (necessary) living expenses.

2. Establish your EMERGENCY SAVINGS account.

3. Establish the amount to be placed in your IN-VESTMENT account.

In the following chapter, I will provide a spreadsheet for you to enter income and expenses to help you set up your savings & investment plan.

**Important Steps in Changing Your Behavior**

• Remember: Do not link debit or credit cards to your savings and investment accounts.

• Immediately establish a firm budget plan, do the work and know how you spend your dollars.

• You should now have developed three plans: 1) your (necessary) living budget 2) your savings plan 3) your investment plan.

*You are now preparing to develop a strategy for building wealth!*

# 3

# BASICS TO RETHINK IN DEVELOPING YOUR SAVINGS & INVESTMENT PLAN

1. **Decide how much money per month you will save** and <u>on what dates</u> depending on your pay schedule (weekly, bi-monthly, or monthly). Be

reasonable and give the amount considerable thought.

2. **Decide how much money will go into each:**

 a) how much to build your SAVINGS account fund for emergencies;

 b) how much for building your INVESTMENT account.

<mark>REMEMBER:</mark> it isn't the size of each of the amounts but the fact that you are getting started.

1. **Don't commit too much or more than you can reasonably afford.** You are just starting your step-by-step path to investing and building wealth. Overcommitting to these funds can cause you to quickly abandon your savings & investment plan in the early stages.

2. **Review your work/earnings schedule.** Does it allow you to consistently save the amounts which you have selected to go into your savings and investment accounts? Do you need to refigure the amounts? Do you need to consider

working longer hours or even a part-time job to meet your savings and investment goals?

2. **Have you thoroughly reviewed your list of expenses** (daily, weekly, monthly) to be certain you have accounted for any expenses which can be removed or reduced? For example, the number of times you or your family dine out per week or month, money that may be thoughtlessly spent out of pocket during the day, unneeded credit or debit card debt, unnecessary clothing expenditures, excessive online shopping, etc.

# Summary

**Carefully reviewing your total plan again is critical to your success.**

This review guards against the possibility of your over or under committing dollars to your total plan!

On the following page, pencil in your monthly budget. Or, visit www.DontDieBroke.net to download the PDF version of this Monthly Budget sheet. On the website, you may also download the Monthly Budget spreadsheet to have your budget calculated automatically. If budget categories specific to you are not listed, feel free to add them. Simply deduct your monthly expenses from your monthly income to determine what is left over to **save and invest**.

# Monthly Budget

## My Monthly Budget

### Monthly income (after taxes)

| | |
|---|---|
| Income/salary from all sources | |
| Investment income | |
| Other income | |
| Savings | |
| Total monthly income | |

**Month:          Year:**

### Monthly expenses

| Home | |
|---|---|
| Mortgage/rent/HOA | |
| Landscaping | |
| Laundry | |
| Gas | |
| Electricity | |
| Water | |
| Home phone (inc. long distance) | |
| Cell phone | |
| Cable | |
| Internet access | |
| Security | |
| | |
| | |
| Total home | |

| Personal | |
|---|---|
| New clothes | |
| Dry cleaning | |
| Salon | |
| | |
| | |
| Total personal | |

| Food | |
|---|---|
| Groceries | |
| Dining out | |
| | |
| | |
| Total food | |

| Auto/transportation | |
|---|---|
| Car loan/lease | |
| Car insurance | |
| Maintenance | |
| Public transit | |
| Parking | |
| Gas | |
| | |
| Total auto/ transportation | |

| Other | |
|---|---|
| Child care | |
| Pet care | |
| | |
| | |
| Total | |

| Health | |
|---|---|
| Toiletries | |
| Cosmetics | |
| Pharmacy | |
| Health club | |
| | |
| | |
| Total health | |

| Entertainment & recreation | |
|---|---|
| Movies | |
| Vacation | |
| Parties/gifts | |
| Subscriptions | |
| | |
| | |
| Total entertainment & recreation | |

| | |
|---|---|
| Total monthly income | |
| - Total monthly expenses | |
| = **Monthly Cash Flow** | |

**Monthly**

| Savings $ | Investment $ |
|---|---|
| | |

© 2019 Borom

# 4

# A STRATEGY TO
# USE IN BUILDING
# YOUR PERSONAL WEALTH

This strategy focuses upon growing your wealth or savings and investments. It will NOT deal with highly sophisticated or more complex investment methods. Those will be left for you to explore once you have developed your basic plan and have the assets available to branch further out.

*At this point, the emphasis is on simplicity.* You may recall the words of Warren Buffett, better known as the **Oracle of Omaha**. In addition to being one of the greatest investors of all time, he has repeatedly recommended that **the safest way for the average investor to build wealth is to invest in index funds on a consistent basis.** Over the years, Buffett's advice has proven to be correct.

This is the pathway that I chose to follow. This is advice I have adhered to very closely in developing my approach to investing.

Although there are no guarantees in the stock market, mutual fund companies that offer index funds are a smart choice that most can follow. Mutual fund company fees for managing the index funds are low, as there is less trading of stocks within the portfolio. Taxes are also lower with this approach.

**Wisely selected index funds usually contain a large number of individual stocks of major companies.** For example, an index fund such as the S&P 500

A STRATEGY TO USE IN BUILDING YOUR PERSONAL WEALTH

(Standard & Poor's 500), includes the stocks of 500 large U.S. companies, including big-name companies such as Apple, Google, Home Depot, Microsoft, and Netflix. If a few of the stocks contained in this or a similar fund underperforms, the other stocks generally perform well enough to keep the fund from losing a significant amount of your money or investment.

**By using index funds**, you are shielded from placing all of your investments into the stock of one company. In essence, **you are decreasing the risk of losing money on your investments.** Also, index funds shield you from the pressure and risk of buying stock in the "right company" because you are basically buying all the companies in an index fund such as the S&P 500.

I am not suggesting that you avoid investing in individual stocks, but that you may want to avoid doing so until you have established a sound investment base made up of index funds. Individual stocks also cost more to manage, which means if you are using an advisor, he or she may take a larger chunk of your earnings.

# Summary

This chapter covered general information about and emphasized the reasons for investing in index funds as a starting point to build your wealth.

## 5

# YOU ARE READY TO DEVELOP YOUR SAVINGS & INVESTMENT PLAN!

**B**ut first, a little education! Please note that I will later list, as examples, just a few of the many mutual fund companies in which you can easily invest your savings.

Let's begin. Let's say, for example, that you have identified the sums of $10 per week for your emergency savings plan and $10 per week for your investment plan. That's $20 per week or $80 per month, or roughly $960 per year. Of this annual sum, $480 would go into your savings emergency fund and $480 into your investment fund.

This is very important. By maintaining the two funds (emergency savings and investment fund), you are protecting yourself from having to dip into your investment fund if an emergency should come up, which requires quick money. Remember to continue to stick to your plan, even if you are thrown a bit off course at times.

**The name of the game is "sticking with your goal of $80 per month."**

For instance, if your monthly savings plan is depleted due to an emergency, continue to maintain your investment plan while rebuilding your savings plan. Do not allow your plan to fall apart, even though you may experience a few difficult times.

Panicking during an emergency and withdrawing all of your investment funds is perhaps the primary reason that most people fail to succeed in developing and maintaining a successful investment plan.

**REMEMBER:** You can always reset your savings and investment goals at a higher or lower level if your situation dictates that you do so. It's important that you DON'T completely abandon your savings and investments.

# Crawl Before You Walk

As you strive to reach your savings goal to allow you to invest in an index fund to build your wealth more rapidly, one possible option is to seek out a bank or credit union which pays the highest available interest rate on your savings.

This permits you to earn a small amount of interest on your savings as you build enough money to invest in mutual funds.

There is also the possibility of placing your savings account in a short-term Certificate of Deposit (CD), which will pay a percent or two higher rate than a regular bank savings account.

CDs can usually be purchased for varying lengths of time, ranging from three months, six months, one year, five years, etc. Do be aware that CDs charge a penalty if you decide to cash them in (withdraw your money) early. However, you may not want to tie up your money for long periods of time, which may prevent you from gaining greater wealth through investing in mutual funds consistently.

Some mutual fund companies offer accounts commonly referred to as "money market funds" which often pay a higher percent of interest (currently 2% to 2.40%), than your typical bank savings account which pays slightly under or over 1%. You may decide to keep all or at least a part of your savings account in your mutual fund "money market" account to earn more interest on your money.

This method would lessen the need for placing all of your savings in an ordinary bank, credit union, or CD account. Plus, it would make it much simpler to directly transfer funds within your mutual fund accounts when you wish to buy additional shares.

However, mutual fund money market accounts generally recommend that you limit the number of checks written on such accounts and limit check amounts to, for example, $250. This is designed to prevent subscribers from treating the money market account as they would a frequently used checking account at a bank of their choice.

**NOTE:** Do not underestimate the power of earning as much as possible on your savings accounts. **Refer to the following paragraph concerning the value of compound interest.** Even seemingly tiny amounts (such as a fraction of one percent), when added up over time, grow far faster than you may think due to the impact of compound interest.

# What is Compound Interest and What is the Value of Compound Earnings on Your Investments?

**Compound interest** (or compounding interest) is interest calculated on the initial principal (money you first invest), which also includes all the accumulated interest of previous periods. **One MUST understand the POWER of compound interest, especially as your money GROWS!**

While most of us understand the interest which a bank or credit union will pay on a typical savings account or CD (around 1% yearly), few of us understand the value of compounded earnings such as interest, dividends, short-term capital gains, and long-term capital gains, that can be earned with your investment in index funds. These items are the money earned from your fund investments which can be automatically *folded* (reinvested) back into the money which you earn on your chosen funds.

51

**This is why you must dedicate yourself to developing an immediate goal of saving in order to start investing in an index fund through a mutual fund company.** In some instances, once you have reviewed your budget, you may find that you can begin both your savings and investment plans immediately.

Again, a term you must always remember is "COMPOUND EARNINGS." Compound earnings happen when the money which your investment funds earned during the year, is credited to the funds or stocks in your investment account. These are the earnings from interest, dividends, short-term capital gains, and long-term capital gains.

I referred to these as automatically reinvested earnings in the paragraph above. Your goal should be to earn an average of 7 - 8% a year once you are invested in index funds.

# 6

# HOW TO MAKE MONEY WHILE YOU SLEEP!

An example: Let's say that you have invested $1,000 for the first year and your index fund earns 8% for the year. I am assuming that a conservative index fund could reasonably return between 7 - 8%. Your $1,000 is now worth $1,080. You earned

$80 on your investment of $1,000. Had the $1,000 earned 1% in a bank savings account or CD, you would have earned $10 in interest for the year.

At the end of the second year, if you had continued to let the $1,080 remain invested in the index fund at 8%, your $1,080 would now be worth $1,166.40. This is before you added an additional $1000 for the second year.

As you can readily see, if the compounding kept occurring year after year or over an extended time, you are going to experience steady progress toward building your wealth and a stable future.

The next example refers to the earlier reference to you saving $960 per year and dividing it into two sections: 1) $480 into your emergency savings account and 2) $480 into your investment account. You would attempt to earn the best interest possible by investing your savings account money through a bank, credit union, CD, or mutual fund "money market" account. However, if you projected 8% earnings on your investment fund of $480.00, you would earn $38.40 for the first year. You would now be worth a total of $518.40.

By investing this amount of $518.40 plus another $480.00 in the second year, you would now be calculating the interest growth on $998.40 x 8%, which would be $79.87 in earned interest and a total two-year return of $118.27. Your two-year investment of $960 would now be worth $1,078.27. **That's the power of compound earnings.**

Better yet, **a picture is worth a thousand words!** If you simply invest $1,000 with no additional investment, on the following page are two charts comparing a 1% vs. 7% rate of return compounded over roughly ten years.

**Chart: Accumulated Return**

Compound interest @ 7%/10 years: $1,000 grows to $2,010

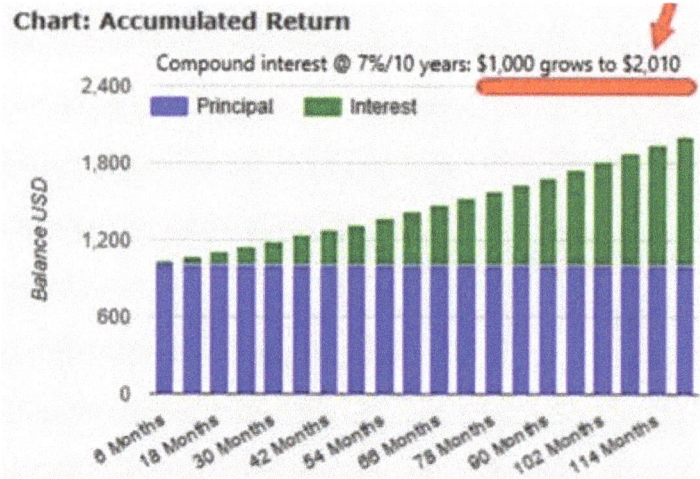

**Chart: Accumulated Return**

Compound interest @ 1%/10 years: $1,000 grows to $1,105

**You are now being paid for having the discipline to invest your money.** You are well on your way to building your wealth. *Make money while you sleep!*

# Summary

I suggest that you grab your calculator. Work out what your investment fund's compounded value would be if you kept your investment going for 3 years, 5 years, 10 years, 15 years, etc. while earning 7 - 8% per year. Or, you can use the Investor.gov Compound Interest Calculator (Google search: *investor.gov compound interest calculator or visit www.DontDieBroke. net to access the calculator*) to do the calculations for you!

The stock market fluctuates, but if you invest for the long-term, your results should approximate those of the fund in which you invest.

# COMPOUND INTEREST CALCULATOR

Determine how much your money can grow using the power of compound interest. Money handed over to a fraudster won't grow and won't likely be recouped. So before committing any money to an investment opportunity, use the "Check Out Your Investment Professional" search tool below the calculator to find out if you're dealing with a registered investment professional.

**\* DENOTES A REQUIRED FIELD**

## Step 1: Initial Investment

**Initial Investment** \*  $1,000

Amount of money that you have available to invest initially.

## Step 2: Contribute

**Monthly Contribution**  $20

Amount that you plan to add to the principal every month, or a negative number for the amount that you plan to withdraw every month.

**Length Of Time In Years** \*  20

Length of time, in years, that you plan to save.

## Step 3: Interest Rate

**Estimated Interest Rate** \*  7

Your estimated annual interest rate.

**Interest Rate Variance Range**

Range of interest rates (above and below the rate set above) that you desire to see results for.

## Step 4: Compound It

**Compound Frequency**  Monthly

Times per year that interest will be compounded.

**CALCULATE**        **RESET**

### Check Out Your INVESTMENT PROFESSIONAL

Individual ▾  Name or CRD#

It's a great first step toward protecting your money. Learn about an investment professional's background, registration status, and more.

*NEVER FORGET THE VALUE OF COMPOUND EARNINGS!*

# 7

# THE NUTS & BOLTS OF CONTINUING YOUR FINANCIAL EDUCATION

A s I stated earlier, don't let the size of the amount of money needed to invest in index funds or stocks overwhelm you.

# The Nuts & Bolts

When you begin investigating mutual fund companies, you will notice that some require a minimum initial investment of $1,000 to $3,000.

However, you should be aware that there are various mutual fund companies which will permit you to start investing for as little as $5 per month or less. Later, I will list some of these companies and contact information for your benefit.

If you have a bank account, most mutual fund companies will permit you to establish an automatic deduction (a link for withdrawal) from your checking or savings bank account with the investment company which you have selected. This feature relieves you of the burden of personally forwarding checks every month to the company.

THE NUTS & BOLTS OF CONTINUING YOUR FINANCIAL EDUCATION

**PLEASE NOTE:** Automatic monthly withdrawals allow you to take advantage of the ability to buy stocks when the stock market falls or when stocks are cheaper, as opposed to always buying stocks when stock prices are consistent or rising. This also means that you are not worrying about timing the market or trying to buy stocks based upon the "ups" or "downs" of the market.

The mutual fund companies make it very easy for you to invest your money to grow your wealth. Can it get any easier to build an investment fund on a steady basis?

# "The best time to plant a tree was 20 years ago. The second-best time is now."

*- Chinese Proverb*

**Remember, your goal is to <u>get started investing</u>.** Again, this means that you <u>start with small steps</u>. By continuing to gradually invest over time, you will be able to grow the size of your investment. As your investment grows, you will be better able to invest in different index funds. This is when you will be able to diversify or increase the number of funds in which you can invest your money. Remaining true to your investment goal is a must. Again, many mutual fund companies will be most helpful to you in making your selections.

# Increase as You Go!

An essential fact to keep in mind is that as you stick to your savings/investment goals, you will probably find yourself in a position to gradually increase the amounts which you can contribute to your plan on a weekly, bi-monthly, monthly, semi-annual, or annual basis.

Such amounts can be realized through small, incremental pay raises, bonuses, income tax refunds, inheritances, part-time work, etc. Please note that these items represent key steps in increasing your wealth.

## Free Money (Take Advantage of Matching Funds)!

You may be employed by a company that provides matching funds for your investment plan. This is usually an amount matching from 1% to 3% of the amount which you save from your salary and contribute to the investment plan provided by the company.

Again, this company money is referred to as 'MATCHING FUNDS." Companies often refer to these saving & investment plans as 401(b) plans.

**This is free money** provided by the company and should encourage you to save very aggressively. In short, the more you increase your savings in the investment plan provided by the company, the larger your 1% to 3% matching portion grows over time. Usually, the various companies provide several index funds in which you can invest.

# 8

# LET'S GET STARTED INVESTING! WHO YOU GONNA' CALL?

Here, in this chapter, you will find a list of services which you may find very helpful in getting started with investing. I am listing several mutual fund companies to familiarize you with the types of funds available.

There are many mutual fund investing companies. However, Vanguard, Fidelity, T. Rowe, Price and American Mutual Funds are four of the major companies I have chosen to use as examples. They all sell index mutual funds and Exchange-Traded Funds (ETFs). They also let you purchase individual stocks through BROKERAGE ACCOUNTS which they can establish for you. Many other companies provide similar services on varying levels.

Before listing examples of mutual fund companies in which you can invest, I will recommend an inexpensive magazine you may find useful.

## KIPLINGER'S PERSONAL FINANCE

 A 12-month subscription is roughly $15. You may call them at 800-544-0155 to subscribe.

The *Kiplinger 25 Funds* features the top 25 index funds recommended by Kiplinger. Each month, Kiplinger magazine lists the status of each of the funds and recommends new funds as needed. **The point is that Kiplinger does some of the investment research work for you and provides other investment articles of interest.** I would strongly recommend that you subscribe to Kiplinger's as a "starting point" to assist in educating yourself and building your investment portfolio.

# Major Mutual Fund Company Examples

With the major mutual fund companies, you can call to discuss which index funds the representative recommends to structure your starter portfolio (based on your risk tolerance). The representative can also provide guidance on how to select index funds based on the fund's returns, expense ratios, and performance ratings over time.

## VANGUARD FUNDS

*(the largest mutual fund and stock purchase company)*

Let me disclose that this is the company that I have the greatest familiarity with and have used for many years. Even though I have invested in index funds from several major fund companies, Vanguard was and remains my base. Why? Because I have found Vanguard's total range of services (for example, available assistance) to be quite useful. This is not to imply that other full-service mutual fund companies are not equally as useful.

You can also link withdrawals from your savings or checking account to your Vanguard account. This makes your investment payments easy to accomplish as long as you keep the necessary funds in your bank account.

Please be aware that Vanguard's minimum starting investment is $1,000 and this amount is limited to several select index funds. This required amount may be too high for those of us who are just starting to develop an investment plan. If so, you may wish to consider Vanguard for future investing when you have built up your investment funds.

Application Information:

1) complete online or 2) request by mail

Vanguard contact information:

1-800-284-7245 or www.vanguard.com

## FIDELITY

*(a large mutual fund and stock purchase company that is excellent for beginning investors)*

Advantage of Fidelity Funds: Fidelity permits you to **start by purchasing one (1) share of any fund.** After that, you can invest any amount at any time (starting at one dollar, five dollars, ten dollars, etc.) per month in its many index funds, four of which are ZERO expense ratio index mutual funds. **This offers a TREMENDOUS OPPORTUNITY** to a beginning or even an established investor.

You can also link withdrawals from your savings or checking account to your Fidelity account. This makes your investment payments easy to accomplish as long as you keep the necessary funds in your bank account.

This opportunity permits any investor to build a diversified portfolio over time that could include several types of index funds. It also allows you to build an investment portfolio, even if you feel that you don't have a huge amount to invest or if you desire to invest a certain amount monthly in selected funds.

Application Information:

1) complete online or 2) request by mail

Fidelity contact information:

1-800-343-3548 or www.fidelity.com

LET'S GET STARTED INVESTING! WHO YOU GONNA' CALL?

## T. ROWE PRICE

*(a large mutual fund and stock purchase company)*

Minimum investment amount for index funds and Exchange-Traded Funds (ETFs) is $2,500. Minimum amount for an IRA (Individual Retirement Account funds) is $1,000. You can also link your investment withdrawals to your bank account. I also have fund investments with T. Rowe Price.

Application information:

1) complete online 2) request by mail

T. Rowe Price contact information:

1-800-537-1936 or www.troweprice.com

## AMERICAN MUTUAL FUNDS

Minimum amount required to invest in any index fund is $250. This amount makes it much easier to invest in some very solid funds sponsored by the company. You may also link to your bank account for automatic contributions.

Application information:

1) complete online 2) request by mail

American Funds contact information:

1-800-421-4225 or www.americanfunds.com

*The following mutual fund companies specialize in algorithmic portfolio managed index funds primarily offering robo-advisors to guide your investment choices:*

## BETTERMENT, LLC

Betterment is a robo-advisor automated fund company that offers low-cost Exchange-Traded Funds (ETFs). **A minimum investment of $10 will open an account. You can open an account with no dollars down before beginning to invest.** All investments are made online and this is a relatively painless way to invest and grow your wealth. Betterment also offers socially responsible portfolios. If opening a basic account, there is a fee to consult with an advisor.

Application information:

Must be completed online at www.betterment.com

Betterment contact information:

1-646-600-8263 or www.betterment.com/

## WEALTHFRONT

Wealthfront is a robo-advisor automated fund company that offers low-cost Exchange-Traded Funds (ETFs). In addition, the fund currently pays approximately 2% on money held in its cash account prior to investing. Wealthfront does not offer online chat for prospective customers or existing clients.

Application information:  Must be completed online at

www.wealthfront.com

Wealthfront contact info:

www.wealthfront.com (no telephone available)

## STASH

Stash is a robo-advisor automated fund which contains over 40 Exchange-Traded-Funds (ETFs) and **requires a minimum investment of $5.00.** This is an inexpensive way to start investing even though your fund selection may be more limited. Stash will assist you in setting up a link to your savings account for automatic contributions to your stash fund account. **Stash will also automatically credit "spare change" from your linked credit or debit cards to your investment account.**

Application information:

www.stashinvest.com

## ACORN INVESTING

Acorn is an app (robo/automated) that permits you to save your assorted change when you make purchases.

Believe it or not, your loose change can add up to $200 to $400 or more per year. This is a painless way to increase your savings and add to your investments, even though the number of investment funds available is limited. Acorn will assist you to invest your savings in a mixture of five diversified Exchange-Traded Funds (ETFs), through automatic linkage with your savings or checking accounts. Acorn automatically **takes your loose change from each credit or debit card purchase and then credits it to your investment account.**

Application information:

www.acorn.com

## ROBINHOOD

Robinhood is a **commission-free (robo-advisor automated) app and has a "0" dollar minimum investment.** Robinhood will invest your savings in ETFs (exchange-traded-funds), stocks and options. Automatic linkage with your savings or checking account can also be established. Again, this is a relatively painless way to invest and grow your wealth.

Application information:

www.robinhood.com

There are many mutual fund companies, but I have limited this review to a few of the major ones which I feel are prominent in the mutual fund investment field.

I included Betterment, Wealthfront, Stash, Acorn, and Robinhood because each represents the more recent movement towards algorithmic portfolio managed investment fund companies offering primarily robo-advisors with digital first approaches, which is good for younger investors. Vanguard, Fidelity, T. Rowe Price, and American Funds represent fully diversified full-service companies that provide numerous services.

Given the amount that you decide to invest, you could invest in several different index funds at the same time as you gain more knowledge. This allows you to diversify among your investments. Again, this is a relatively painless way to invest and grow your wealth.

If you prefer verbally discussing your investing direction, the major mutual fund companies are critical in reaching your savings & investment goals. The efficient and helpful level of service which full service mutual fund companies provide will pleasantly surprise you. They truly serve to assist you in building your wealth through investing your money. You will be pleased with the knowledge and results which you will gain from interacting with these types of companies.

*These companies are beginning to enter the robo-advisor field. If interested, ask if they are offering this service or any other similar services for beginning investors.*

*Please keep in mind that financial service offerings constantly change over time. Be sure to ask the mutual fund company representatives for any updates to the above listed information.*

# 9

# KEEP IT SIMPLE

**Y**ou may find it easier to place your investment money with one full-service mutual fund company. This provides a single source for providing you with a monthly report of your investments. As such, this makes understanding and keeping up with your investments much easier.

*Please note, I would strongly recommend that you avoid working with individual stocks and options at this stage of your investment journey.*

Targeted Retirement Funds (TRFs)

**SPECIAL INFORMATION:** If you want a relatively easy and safer entry point to start your investment program, consider placing your initial investment money in a Targeted Retirement Fund (TRF). Targeted Retirement Funds are provided by most of the full-service fund companies such as Vanguard, Fidelity, T. Rowe Price, etc.

Targeted Retirement Funds can be matched to your future retirement date/age and generally yield or pay between 6% to 8% per year. TRFs hold a mixture of stocks and bonds which are selected by the company which sponsors the fund.

In this way, you are not forced to attempt to select from a large variety of index funds on your own or risk placing your money in another type of single fund which may not do as well. Once you have established a fund of this type, you can branch off later into different index funds as your knowledge and investment money increases.

# Summary

**NOTE:** For the sake of clarification, let me state a simple difference between index funds and Exchange-Traded Funds (ETFs) funds. ETFs are more liquid, can be traded frequently throughout the day, have lower-cost fees, and generally have a lower total cost of ownership. ETF expense fund rates generally run from 0.7 to 0.15 in fees. This rate is sourced from the Betterment Retirement Portfolio for 2018.

Index funds can only be traded once per day which limits their liquidity and they generally charge higher fees. However, during the past several years, index funds have been rapidly lowering the cost of fees. Many now match the fees charged by ETFs.

**KEY COMMENT:** Once you've started your savings and investment plan, stick with it through your challenges and the fluctuation of the stock market. As time passes, you'll see results.

**Long-term investing is like gardening.** You would not plant seeds and dig them up to start over if you did not see a full-grown plant in the first month. The same applies to investing – it's a garden. Be patient and let your money grow.

**As your investment knowledge increases over time, you will also improve your investment skills!**

# Happy Budgeting!
# Happy Saving!
# Happy Investing!

**PLANT YOUR GARDEN AND WATCH IT GROW!**

# ACKNOWLEDGEMENTS FROM THE AUTHOR

In writing this brief and hopefully easily digestible book, I feel compelled to acknowledge my thanks and gratitude to you, the reader.

There are three reasons for doing so:

- I can empathize and actually feel the anxiety each of you has felt or is currently feeling with regard to financial investing.

- I have been driven to share with you my various learning experiences, which so many of us encounter as we try to obtain a basic understanding of financial investments. I hope the experiences I have shared with you make your path to building your wealth easier.

- I credit you, the reader, with having given me the purpose and momentum to assist you in reversing the tremendous INEQUALITY in the distribution of wealth in our world.

I would also like to thank my devoted son R. T. Borom for his unflagging enthusiasm in bringing Don't Die Broke to publication.

*R. L. Borom*

# ACKNOWLEDGEMENTS FROM THE AUTHOR

It is an honor to collaborate on this book with my father. I would like to thank him for his love, wisdom and unfailing desire to make this world a better, kinder, and more equitable place in which to live. I give thanks to God for His grace, my mother, my wife and sons, my brother and my sister, Denise F. for her expert publishing guidance, IngramSpark, Lauren P., Lisa D., James P. O'Day (CPA), The Sea Cliff Bistro (for those early morning cups of Joe, choice table, and good vibes during the red-eyed editing sessions!) and you, the reader, for inspiring me to make this world a better place for our children and future generations. Build your wealth!

*R. T. Borom*

# FOOTNOTES

[1]*Bloomberg Businessweek, May 27, 2019, p, 47*

[2]*Millions of Americans are Left Out of the Stock Market Boom*, CNN Business, October 20, 2017

# Each one teach one!

# CREDITS

Editing and illustration selection by R. T. Borom/Pigs Fly High, Inc. Publishing

Layout design by 5mediadesign

Cover concept by R. T. Borom & cover design by Kiryl

Calm Pig Photo by Skitterphoto @ Pexels

Bank Banknotes Cash Stacked Bills Photo by Pixabay from Pexels

Stay Focused Photo by rawpixel.com from Pexels

Education Exam Hand Photo by Louis Bauer @ Pexels

Caffeine Cards Coffee Beans Photo by Lukas @ Pexels

By Cash Coins Pig Photo by Skitterphoto @ Pexels

Apple Brainstorm Camera Photo by rawpixel.com from Pexels

Calculating Challenge Chess Champion Photo by Pixabay from Pexels

Adorable-Baby-Beautiful-Girl by Angeliz Olivares from Pexels

Asian Boys Community Photo by Kat Wilcox from Pexels

Two Adults Blurred Background Daylight Photo by RUN 4 FFWPU from Pexels

Beautiful Beauty in Bed Photo by Bruce Mars from Pexels

Bolts Chrome Fastener Photo by Pixabay from Pexels

Asian Bride and Groom Photo by Mentadgt from Pexels

Cash Cent Child Piggy Bank Photo by rawpixel from Pexels

Group of Four People Holding Speech Boxes Photo by rawpixel from Pexels

Asphalt Aspiration Clouds Photo by Gratisography from Pexels

Bank Notes Garden Photo by Pixabay from Pexels

Green Pig Photo by Alexas_Fotos from Pixabay

# FEEDBACK

Thank you for purchasing and reading **Don't Die Broke**. I hope my life experiences and research gave you insight into the world of saving, investing, and building wealth.

If you enjoyed reading this book, I would appreciate if you could leave a review on Amazon.

Feedback from my readers and reviews on Amazon, do make a difference. I read all the reviews and would like to hear your thoughts. Thank you!

*R. L. Borom*

# FULL DISCLAIMER

Neither Pigs Fly High, Inc., nor any of its directors, officers, shareholders, personnel, representatives, agents, or independent contractors (collectively, the "Operating Parties") nor R. L. Borom, nor R. T. Borom, shall be held liable or responsible for any damage you may suffer as a result of either failing to independently research, perform due diligence and/or personally consider and analyze your financial circumstances, or failing to seek competent advice from an independent financial professional who is familiar with your situation, prior to taking any action in making an investment decision or otherwise.

The material in this book may include information, products, or services by third parties. Third party material is comprised of the products, opinions, and services offered or expressed by their owners. As such, the author of this book does not assume responsibility for any third-party material or opinions.

The publishing of such third-party material does not constitute the author's guarantee of any information, instruction, opinion, products, or services contained within the third-party materials. Use of recommended third party material does not guarantee that your results will mirror those of the author. Publication of such third-party material is simply a recommendation and expression of the author's own opinion of that material.

Great effort has been made to safeguard the accuracy of this writing. Opinions expressed in this book have been formulated as a result of research, personal experience as well as the experiences of others. Any questions or comments regarding the Disclaimer for *Don't Die Broke*, please contact the publisher, Pigs Fly High, Inc., at pigsflyhighinc@gmail.com.

## YOUR NOTES

# DON'T DIE BROKE

## Easy Steps on How to Save, Invest, and Build Your Wealth

Published by

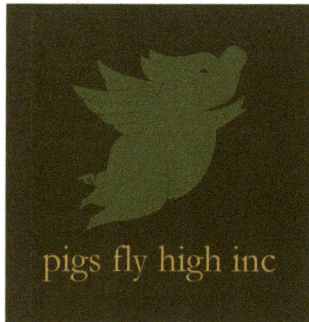

pigs fly high inc

Contact: pigsflyhighinc@gmail.com

Visit the www.DontDieBroke.net blog for investing

tips and additional ways to build your wealth!

www.ingramcontent.com/pod-product-compliance
Lightning Source LLC
Chambersburg PA
CBHW040906210326
41597CB00029B/4990